Dearest Harry
With all my love
John

WILSON'S ANGLE

JOHN WILSON

Boxtree

First published in 1990
by Boxtree Limited.

British Library Cataloguing in Publication Data
Wilson, John, 1943 July 24 –
   Wilson's Angle.
   1. Angling
   I. Title
   799.12
   ISBN 1–85283–296–7

Edited by Janita Clamp

Designed by Dave Goodman/Millions Design

Typeset by Cambrian Typesetters, Frimley, Surrey

Printed and bound in Italy by OFSA S.p.A.
for Boxtree Limited,
36 Tavistock Street,
London. WC2E 7PB

CONTENTS

FOREWORD AND DEDICATION

THERE ARE MANY DIFFERENT INFLUENCES WHICH SHAPE THE LIFE OF A fisherman and as the seasons and years pass I feel more and more strongly the urge to capture and preserve on film a record of these. The photographs in this book are a selection, chosen because they are favourites of mine, but I hope that they will bring equal pleasure to the reader.

Young fishermen today are influenced most strongly by television and video, but my childhood days in the 1950's belong most of all to Bernard Venables whose wonderful cartoon strip, *Mr Crabtree Goes Fishing* motivated and instructed an entire generation of anglers. It is to Bernard Venables that I dedicate this book, to say thank you for providing so many with such a broad outlook, not just on fishing but on the countryside as well.

My appreciation also goes to friends who suffer my direction as I photograph them and who patiently endure my instructions when I give them the camera to photograph me. To Andy Davison, Doug Allen, Jinx Davey, Martin Founds, Bruce Vaughan, Charlie Clay and others, thank you.

John Wilson
Great Witchingham 1990

NATURE AND THE STREAM

STREAMS ARE WHERE CHILDREN BECOME FISHERMEN. Amid the surroundings of clear running water and lush, dense undergrowth, an apprenticeship in natural history begins. Mysterious, oily depths beneath the boles of gnarled trunks, or narrow runs between tall beds of dark green bullrush stems, always hold the promise of a chub or two, while rapidly flowing funnels of shallow, well-oxygenated water attract dace or brown trout.

Crawling slowly on all fours through the aroma of crushed water mint to approach a crafty chub, or viewing the occupants of a deep clear glide from the branches of an over-hanging willow, you are commando, naturalist, tree-climber and fisherman rolled into one. Stealth is all-important, and the human frame adapts quickly, learning the advantage of using local cover, of carrying the minimum of tackle and using natural baits.

By all means take along slices of bread, worms or maggots but should you forget them, there are plenty of naturals either in or beside the stream. Slugs from the wet grass, big worms from under fallen logs, caterpillars, spiders, grasshoppers, dock grubs or elderberries. All are freely abundant.

WILSON'S ANGLE

FAR AWAY FROM FARMING CHEMICALS, NATURE and the stream create perfect conditions for a wealth of wild flowers with perfumes which could never be manufactured. Colours, mostly shades of pastel, surround the enquiring angler as he wanders, arms held high to evade the bite of nettles, beside parts of a diminutive course rarely trodden by others.

Naturally the most overgrown areas provide the very best fishing, to those who walk slowly and stealthily and polaroid glasses are essential to diminish surface glare – almost as important as the bait itself. Also necessary are waterproof trousers or long boots for kneeling down below the skyline when short-range fishing. One careless footfall, one shadow cast over the gin clear water, quickly puts an end to any action from that swim. But don't be discouraged, you soon come to appreciate that streaming is a roving pursuit. Besides, few spots will contain enough fish to warrant the use of a stool. So enjoy the freedom of movement and explore the twisting and turning course with its overgrown mystery and challenge around every corner.

Down on the bottom of the stream clinging to the undersides of large flints or sodden timber, the caddis grub lives a sedentary life protected in a case which it constructs from tiny bits of wood, stone and sand particles. Several dozen of these succulent baits can be collected in a few minutes and kept moist till required in damp moss. Pinch the tail gently for the head to appear, whereupon the grub, larvae of the sedge fly, may be eased from its house by the legs. Twice the size of any maggot, the caddis grub is a bait relished by fish living in both still and running water.

OF ALL THE SPECIES LIVING IN CLEAN, RUNNING WATER DACE OFFER THE MOST consistent sport. Even tiny streams where the roach and chub reach only modest proportions have the capacity to breed dace weighing up to the pound. Is this because dace take best advantage of the available food source, or is the growth of larger species restricted by the size of the stream? It is an interesting phenomenon.

Carrying nothing more than a few short, stumpy floats plus shots and hooks you can search each and every type of swim: long-trotting the shallow glides, holding the bait back so that it waves enticingly upwards at the tail-end of turbulent pools, or simply using the weight of the bait itself to 'freeline' beneath low branches. This is stream fishing at its best.

NATURE AND THE STREAM

CONCEALMENT, ACCURATE CASTING AND OBSERVA-tion are just a few of the techniques necessary for sorting out the larger roach – by far the wiliest of stream dwellers. Adult roach rarely show the bold, careless gluttony of the chub, or compete for food with the eagerness of dace. If they cannot find the protection of a long, deep-water run, they seek the shelter of cover above. Dense overhanging willows or alders are much favoured, particularly where flotsam collects on the surface to form a raft over-head. The quiet darkness of such jungle swims is comforting to big roach.

Once a handful of specimens have been visually located or are suspected in a promising run, fishing quietly on into dusk as light comes off the surface will increase the chances of success. A thumbnail piece of fresh white breadflake hiding a size 10 hook tied direct to 3 lbs test, and laid gently on the bottom with small shot above, or simply freelined through the swim, will do nicely. A big worm will occasionally sort out a large stream roach, especi-ally following heavy rain when thousands get washed into streams from the land. Heavy bombs and complicated ledger rigs are not worth the effort, and light values are far more important than expensive bite indicators. Simply keep a bow in the line from rod tip to surface and watch for that positive 'tightening' (or sudden 'slack liner' should the roach swim upstream instead of down), as a fish confidently sucks in the bait.

When darkness falls and the line becomes difficult to see, just when the largest roach of all start to feed, simply hook it over the index finger and feel for bites – it can be a magical sensation.

WILSON'S ANGLE

AS THE YEAR 2000 APPROACHES, THE BIGGEST THREAT TO OUR RIVERS AND streams, and by extension our drinking water, is pollution. This is not just the overt industrial pollution we used to see – detergent foam covering the surface of the water – but the insidious leakage of silage and chemicals from farmland. It will continue until government and EEC policies are drastically changed. The River Authorities too, often pollute the fisheries they are supposed to be protecting through inadequate and outdated sewerage control.

Very much alone in the fight against river pollution is the Anglers Cooperative Association, the only independent organisation committed to restoring contaminated fisheries and prosecuting the polluter under common law. Under the directorship of Alan Edwards, (who I had the privilege of interviewing during the filming of an episode of *Go Fishing*), the A.C.A. is asking for the support of everyone, not only anglers but every member of the public who cares about the future of our waterways.

AGGRESSIVE PREDATORS

THERE IS NO BETTER LIVING EXAMPLE OF THE saying 'Nature red in tooth and claw' than the freshwater pike. The pike is hardly coy about its carnivorous habits and is without question the most effective subsurface predator. Like all carrion-eaters, pike, especially big pike, live very comfortably off the natural abundance of sickly, dying or dead fish. One of the main reasons why dead fish are rarely seen upon the surface (except in cases of pollution) is because the pike, like the wolf, can sense a creature in trouble and dispose of it quickly. It is for this reason that static deadbait, lying completely inert upon the bed of a lake or river, is so effective in landing bigger than average size pike. This is not to deny that spinners, plugs, livebaits and even wobbled deadbaits take their fair share, and each on its day will outfish static deadbaits, but overall, the freshly killed static deadbait is the most effective. It is its obvious availability which makes it more liable to be seen by larger, more lethargic pike, than other offerings. Moreover it is not going to get away, or outrun a fat old pike as a lively bait or a lure worked too fast through heavily coloured water might.

THAT *ESOX LUCIOUS* HAS THE JAW CAPACITY TO make short work of even a 2 lbs fish there is no doubt. Even with specimens in excess of that magical 20 lbs mark, immense problems are created on the strike when trying to set the hooks, and especially when casting such large baits. Monstrous pike however, do not necessarily result from monstrous deadbaits. What is important is that the bait lies in a natural manner on the bottom. For instance, to counterbalance the pull of hooks, trace or weights so that bait hangs above dense bottom weeds, a foam strip or an injection of air is the answer. It is the sight of a natural-looking, easy meal which makes deadbaits so attractive to big pike, not the actual size. It doesn't even matter what the deadbait happens to be – any sea or freshwater fish up to seven or eight inches long, offered either as whole or half baits, will take large pike. If the added attraction of natural colour is available, for instance a dead goldfish from the garden pond, red mullet or other exotic reef fishes, so much the better. Of course, any silver-sided fish may easily be dyed.

A freshly-killed mouse or rat deposited at the front door by the family cat, a chunk of liver from the local butcher's shop, an octopus or squid, all these are potential pike baits. Don't write anything off until its possibilities have been explored. Scavenging pike can be as finicky about their meal as the most uncooperative carp when it suits them. Then again on the very next occasion they will devour anything in their path – even commonplace baits badly presented on tackle more suited to shark fishing. But that's life.

THE SURVIVAL INSTINCTS OF ALL ANIMALS EQUIP THEM TO RECOGNISE DANGER, either instinctively or by experience, and fish are no exception. However some theories of modern pike fishing appear to disregard this, arguing that a pike is incapable of remembering the species of fish or type of artificial lure with which it was last caught. Foolishly they offer the same old baits or artificials, in the same manner, in the same lake, week after week and wonder why their catch rate deteriorates, leading to the inevitable 'blank sessions' even under ideal water and weather conditions.

The cynics might suggest that artificial lures are created by manufacturers to catch fisherman rather than fish, but only penny-pinching pike fishermen really believe this. The success of an effective lure is that it provokes aggression; plugs in particular really turn pike on and because there are so many variants, from the gurgling and spluttering surface attractors, to the big-lipped, floating divers, the same area may be systematically covered till a 'taking' lure is found.

Who knows why on the day, a particular plug of a certain colour seems to outfish the rest? Is it visibility, water colour, depth, weed-growth, temperature, air-pressure, shoal-fish availability? Only the pike knows, thank goodness.

IT IS NO SECRET THAT WATER TEMPERATURE HAS A DIRECT BEARING ON THE feeding and fight of most freshwater fish, in particular aggressive species such as pike. With the onset of winter when day or night temperatures are around the freezing mark, their metabolism slows right down; pike feed less frequently, take longer to swallow their prey and their spectacular warm weather fighting spirit is considerably dampened. Why then is pike fishing considered by some to be a winter pursuit? It is true that during the coldest weather the chances of latching onto a really big fish are greater when, along with carp, pike slow down to a crawl, but for both these species the best sport is to be had during the summer months. It is during this season that the fisherman may experience the never to be forgotten exhilaration of a pike running for freedom, cavorting high into the air to tail walk across the surface in an effort to eject the bait.

DESPITE THE RAW BEAUTY OF A BROADLAND sunset, being out alone in a rocking boat as chill replaces the soft afternoon light can prove a fruitless pursuit. Does the outside chance of a huge pike happening along to snaffle up one of the dead-baits before total darkness closes in, really make the decision to stay put worthwhile? If you're wrong and there is no further action, it's a long, lonely row back.

There is no hard and fast rule concerning when pike will feed; they will feed all day long if the mood and the wind suit them. North-westerlies or cold north winds may only prompt one or two fish into movement at first light, at midday when the sun is at its highest, or strangely also at dusk when temperatures fall sharply. If there has been no action all day it is likely that something will happen at dusk. But if the pike has already fed and moved with the wind you could sit there until dawn with no results. It is impossible to predict.

On hard-fished waters it is night fishing without doubt that can prove worthwhile. Whether the water is a river, pit, or broad, prebaiting with deadbaits every night or so for a few weeks, brings rich rewards on that first night session. Like all fish, pike respond to a regular source of free food. Even those well-used suspicious baits, which would certainly be ignored during the day, are snapped up without hesitation under the cloak of darkness.

However, there are drawbacks. For the pike enthusiast who revels in watching the line hiss through the water, or great tail patterns come boiling to the surface from several feet down, pike fishing in the darkness is just not the same.

AGGRESSIVE PREDATORS

THE PIKE WITH ITS AWESOME DENTAL ARMORY IS WITHOUT DOUBT THE MOST voracious of predators, but trout, from the humble brookie to the North American laker (which can top 60 lbs), must come a very close second. Their swallowing power is quite incredible. They can switch at a moment's notice from attacking the largest of spoons to delicately sipping in aquatic larvae, and it is this versatility which makes the species so interesting and such a challenge. Trout can prove devastatingly easy to catch or despairingly hard, especially when they become entirely preoccupied with a particular form of minute aquatic life. It is because trout are sometimes just too greedy for their own good, with eyes much larger than their bellies that man has been forced into creating rules for their preservation.

The trout is a true cold water species and only during bouts of humid weather and high water-temperature does its aggression and willingness to feed ever seem to wane, in all other conditions it is to the trout's aggressive streak that attack must be geared. Young fishermen prefer twitched worms or spinners – both extremely effective – while the 'limit' fisherman's wallet is crammed with gaudy creations (few representing any real forms of life) which have been designed to incite rage or territorial aggression.

AS THE MASSIVE PIKE IS HAULED OVER THE gunnel, its glistening olive livery heavily spotted in cream, only strained arm muscles and the obvious immense width across the creature's back hint that this is no scrawny twenty pounder. Only when it is finally laid in the bottom of the boat, protected from its own strength on a piece of old carpet or underlay, can its true bulk be assessed. Surely one of the magical moments of fishing is when that needle swings round to the 30 lbs mark.

But fishing should never only be about trophies. Go for them by all means, but at the same time enjoy the bonuses that accompany fishing even when trophies are hard to come by. The bite of early morning frost in the nostrils, the thrill of anticipation as the boat is loaded in the mist of dawn and items on the mental checklist are ticked off: the pair of mudweights, waterproofs, tool kit for the outboard engine, the box of dead baits. It is a worthwhile exercise – there's nothing worse than realising you've forgotten something vital, two miles down river. Then take time to sit quietly and watch the heron that takes to the air, its breakfast interrupted, and the tiny black spiders that seem to create themselves out of the mist to string minute webs across the river, which attach your anchored boat to the reedy shore. Notice the sound and sight of a flight of ducks who pass low overhead because they know that the angler rarely carries a gun. On the slow days, and to the winter pike fisherman these can be many, it is sights, sounds and sensations such as these which replace the elation of big fish triumph, and which contribute to the store of memories that any fisherman treasures.

BOTH PERCH AND TROUT LIVE AT GREAT DEPTHS and feed on a diet consisting largely of smaller fishes. Lacking crunching, killing teeth, they quickly gulp in and swallow their prey. However, they do differ in one important and fundamental way: perch cannot equalise pressure when being wound vertically to the surface from deep water because they have closed air bladders. Like the deep-sea diver who surfaces too quickly, perch all too easily suffer from the bends and often never recover.

The reason for this lies in the air bladder which is situated against the backbone, and in which gases expand or contract. In the case of the trout, a pneumatic duct connects the air bladder to the alimentary canal which means that the fish is able to release the pressure from rapidly expanding gases by 'passing wind' as it is played to the surface. Great clusters of bubbles, rising ahead of a fish is a common sight, especially when bringing up a trout from the deep water lakes of North America. The perch is without this pneumatic duct and no one is yet sure to what depths it can withstand vertical ascent without suffering fatally. Even fifteen or twenty feet may be too much if the fish is being cranked up quickly.

It may be for this reason that on most deep lakes and pits, sport with big perch never seems to last more than a season or two, once their existence becomes common knowledge to fishermen. Whether this is because the fish die after being released or because they recover and become extra crafty, never falling for the baited hook again, is matter for endless speculation.

SUMMER
DELIGHT

A GLORIOUS SUNRISE IS A TREASURED EXPERIENCE FOR ANYONE, AND FOR those who go out especially early in order to sit beside dew-soaked rushes and watch the sun appear from darkness over the horizon, the experience is even more magical. Man's latent primitive hunting instinct, subdued by modern living, is stirred as he realises that if he lets his eyes become accustomed he doesn't need a torch to see in the dark. After all, why should human beings not possess an ability shared by all other living creatures? Hearing too, although tuned to the sounds of the technological world, does not take long to adjust to a whole new range of sounds during night fishing: the crackling of dry leaves as a toad crawls clumsily along, the whirring flight of a roosting pheasant as it leaves its perch, the sucking of carp as they slurp amongst surface scum, the unbelievable racket made by a badger foraging through dense undergrowth.

While the night is full of a thousand sounds, the dawn brings colour and a sense of promise. Great bronze backs gradually become visible as they break surface in the gently rising mist, while long streams of bubbles spew and turn to froth along the water's edge. A leviathan catapults itself vertically into the air to shake the parasites from its gills before crashing noisily back into the depths. The natural world offers all these sensory experiences, and as the pace of modern life becomes more frantic, they are all the more precious. What more could the fisherman ask in exchange for a few hours lost sleep?

SUMMER DELIGHT

'SMALL WATERS, BIG FISH' IS NOT SIMPLY A USEFUL yardstick, it is a statement of fact. Enormous eels lurk in the tiniest of farm ponds which never see the bait of a serious angler. Feeding on a rich diet of crustacea and small fishes, an eel can grow for 20 years or more before the urge to breed takes it overland and downstream through a network of rivers, to its eventual spawning ground in the Sargasso Sea.

It is hard to believe that eels travel overland from remote ponds, through wet grass to join river systems, but they do. This journey can take place only during the hours of darkness and in torrential rain and is therefore never witnessed. But who ever sees moles mating, or the nest of a skylark, or the enigmatic brook lamprey attached to a stone by its circular mouth? Yet the existence of all these things is believed and taken for granted just as the strange journey of the eel should be. The proof, if needed, manifests itself when in the dead of night the indicator rises positively to the butt ring, line evaporates from the spool and a creature weighing anything from three to ten pounds, which started its life as a three inch elver drifting towards our shores with the trade winds, swims back to its lair with your bait.

SUMMER DELIGHT

WHEN DUCKS GO INTO ECLIPSE — THAT PERIOD OF moulting during the summer months — it is difficult to tell drakes from ducks until they feather up again for mating. But not so with the tench. More than any other species of freshwater fish, the characteristic difference between the sexes is plainly obvious all year through. It is not just the rounded figure of the female tench against the much smaller male, which aids instant recognition. The pelvic fins too provide precise sexing. The lady possesses neat, almost pointed pelvics which never cover the vent, lying flat to her belly whether swollen with spawn or not. The male tench have enormous 'crinkly' spoon-shaped pelvic fins, which completely cover the vent, almost touching the leading edge of the anal fin when lying flat. In addition, males sport pronounced muscle lumps on both flanks immediately above the pelvics.

At certain times of the year, at prespawning and shortly afterwards, segregration of the sexes is a noticeable phenomenon. It is not uncommon to catch a dozen or more fish which turn out to be either all males or all females, although this probably happens with other species which are hard to sex, such as perch, zander and pike.

A knowledge of the size to which male tench may grow is of considerable value to the specialist angler. In small overstocked lakes or pits where the males rarely top two or three pounds, the chances of landing a spawned-out female with a natural weight in excess of 5–6 lbs are slim. But where male tench are regularly caught weighing over 4½ lbs or even 5 lbs, the top female weight could be anything between 7–9 lbs.

THE DELIGHTS OF SUMMER COME IN MANY DIFFERENT and often surprising forms; from long hard battles with seemingly tireless carp, to the chance meeting with a freshwater rarity. One such rarity, coloured more like a banana than the real thing – even down to the black flecks – is the unusual golden tench. With pointed fins distinctly tinged in pink and a bright black eye, golden tench are in a class of their own, even as ornamentals.

Strange really that nature should sanction such easy prey, or do we blame man's eternal fascination with genetics? Either way, since it rarely exceeds more than 3 lbs, fishermen value its colour more than its fighting prowess.

ON THE FACE OF IT SWANS AND LARGE ROACH WOULD seem to have little in common, but closer observation reveals that they share many similarities. Both thrive in clean running water with abundant vegetation, both feed at depths of between two and five feet where pickings are richest, both are attracted to the angler's bait and both are beautiful.

An adult specimen roach with its vermillion fins and silvery blue back is the float fisherman's most prized trophy and certainly his hardest won. But in catching one beautiful creature to admire, we must ensure that we do not in the process cause lasting harm to another.

When a swan is feeding in the 'bottoms up' position, its extending neck means that it is foraging along the river bed to a depth of four and five feet, at the mercy of any discarded line or tackle. As the threat of fatal leadshot has diminished, the swan's safety can be further assured if unwanted terminal tackle is taken home and disposed of.

SUMMER DELIGHT

WITH SCALES IN IRIDESCENT HUES OF SILVER, pewter and white, its fins tinged with yellow, what fisherman ever dreamt of catching such a carp?

The origins of the carp date back to the ancient Chinese and Japanese empires, where they were bred for food and colour selection rather than sport. It is only since the 1980s that British anglers have had the pleasure of catching these stunning fish.

Crossing the beauty of the koi, which to the Japanese symbolises strength, masculinity and love, with one of the broad-shouldered, fast-growing strains of European carp which are cultured specifically for their table qualities, produces these resilient hard-fighting variants, which add a valuable dimension to carp fishing.

The desire to catch larger and larger fish is a natural trap, into which we all fall. But these tinted newcomers, available in all the scale patterns of uncoloured carp, give anglers a new goal; a creature which is just as hard to catch but whose unique beauty makes weight of secondary importance. Metallics quickly realise that their colour makes them highly visible and this awareness makes them much harder to catch, particularly on floating baits. Rarely are they to be seen head and shoulders out of the water, boldly gobbling up everything in their path, as pot-bellied naturals might do. Metallics sense their vulnerability when shooting up to the surface and characteristically stand on their tails immediately below the floater for a second or two. They then either suck it in or bolt off in such a swirl that the angler thinks the bait has gone. The limp line between floater and rod however, tells a different story.

SUMMER DELIGHT

JUST AS PINE CONES AND HOAR FROSTS ARE SO characteristic of winter, so lily pads and the beautiful rudd evoke the months of summer. Lovers of warm water in shallow lakes and meres, rudd are seldom far from lilies, which provide both shelter and a rich food source in the snails and eggs which cling to the undersides of the pads. Sure signs of rudd at home are when pads or stalks can distinctly be seen 'knocking'. While the rudd can be a timid biter, a bait offered 'on the drop' between or alongside the pads on completely weightless tackle, will be sucked in with surprising aggression.

Only when alarmed by a careless shadow upon the surface, or by bank vibrations, do shoal fish such as rudd become wary. As one of a large group, their very existence is based upon competition and grabbing food before the next guy. So down below the mass of surface pads where light is diffused and the outside world seems far away, the rudd will succumb even to stout tackle.

Only when winter sets in and the lilies die back does this golden beauty tone down its scales to shades of muted brass. Does the falling water temperature alert the rudd to how conspicuous its bright colours make it without the protection of subsurface greenery and provoke this change? Only nature knows.

PERSONAL
FAVOURITES

WITH SUMMER COME ALL THE BEST THINGS. Sultry evenings and nights when nothing seems to sleep; carp slurp, and swallows and swifts sip in flies on the wing. Gentle dawns break without chill and the surface of the water is latticed with streams of feeding bubbles, a patchwork of frothy tramlines indicating that the carp at least have enjoyed breakfast. Warm hazy days seem full of promise when the quarry can be seen and followed in the clear water.

Inevitably the wandering, opportunist carp man is a successful fisherman. He has to be if only a few hours per session is all that work or family life allows. Besides, catching carp in simple style through observation and stealth opens a picture book of natural history. To drop a freeline bait beside marginal sedges, to manoeuvre the float into gaps between lily pads, or to peer through the network of willow and alder leaves using their canopy as cover, permits breathtakingly close observation. The miracle of viewing huge fish feeding uninhibited through clear water, is unbeatable. There will even be times no doubt, when this experience replaces the hunter's urge to catch; just having been there is satisfaction enough.

AS THE BUOYANT PEACOCK STEM RISES VERTICALLY and topples over, it is only when it lies completely flat that the unsuspecting carp will feel the single shot four inches from the hook. By then it is too late, the float fisherman has already struck, taken a pace backwards, and wound the rod into a full, powerful curve. Against such an elastic spring, the carp's great propeller-like tail has reduced thrust, and the chance that it will reach the sanctuary of dense lilies or a line of sedges is a slim one. The carp is off-balance and therefore controllable.

The same carp hooked on a ledger rig would have shot off in a panic at 20 miles an hour into snags and difficult hiding places from where extraction would be tricky. This alone is good reason for those who capitalise on seeing the feeding bubbles of carp rising to the surface, to assume that 'bugging the bubblers' with float tackle, has no equal.

BIG CARP ACHIEVE THEIR SIZE FEEDING UPON A rich, and extensive diet of natural food. Theirs is the world of mud or silts and the nutrients they contain, from the tiny red-celled blood-worms, (larvae of the midge fly), to larger, more substantial single food items such as freshwater snails, cockles and mussels.

Carp are armed with powerful flat-edged grinding teeth located in the back of their throat, and can easily crunch small molluscs to feed on the succulent meats inside. It is little wonder that the peach-coloured flesh of the giant swan mussel, whose tough shell is not so easily crushed, is quickly devoured when made readily available by the fisherman. For carp, it is the ultimate treat, and for the fisherman, this bait, easily gathered at the waterside in the marginal muds brings welcome rewards. What's more it is entirely free.

The orange 'foot' should be nicked onto a size 4 hook tied direct, and the loose bits may be scattered around as ground bait attractor. There are few waters where the carp will not respond greedily and prebaiting an area for a few days with chopped mussels prior to fishing, can produce quite staggering results.

Not only carp but tench also adore this natural food, as do big roach and rudd; after dark the most likely customers are eels and catfish. However, not all areas around the lake shore will contain mussels in useful numbers. Look for piles of broken mussel shells, either in the shallows or on land, and you will have discovered where the expert Mr. Heron collects *his* mussels. Thank goodness he's such an untidy diner!

CONTEMPLATING THE LIKELIHOOD OF FISH FROM the river at dawn, the fields concreted in white frost accompanied by a biting east wind, is not everyone's idea of chub fishing. As a species chub are far easier to see and to catch during the summer months.

Like the carp, chub also have powerful pharyngeal teeth capable of mashing to a pulp the largest of crayfish or any small fish up to five or six inches long. Huge chub, those weighing 5 lbs and above, have the capacity to swallow much larger fish. Even a dace of fully eight ounces would not be out of the question, particularly during the colder months when normal food sources are rather thin on the ground.

Large baits however, though devastatingly effective at times, do present all kinds of problems with presentation and subsequent hooking. This is why for consistent, cold weather sport with 'old rubber lips', worms, breadflake or crust, or a strong-smelling cheese paste are considered best.

SMALL RIVER CHUBBING RARELY ALLOWS TWO anglers to share the same swim, except when times are hard and bites are few. Then, friends may enjoy locating their quarry by keeping to small, confined areas close to the bank, away from the turbulent main flow, and leap-frogging downstream. The upstream angler presents a shorter line than his downstream partner to save freezing fingers from having to deal with tangles.

This is a wonderful way to turn miserable conditions into an opportunity for friendly conversation while at the same time systematically covering an unfriendly river. While quiver-tipping with a static bait is the necessary technique for both anglers, each can try a different bait, and juggle with terminal rigs until a winning combination is found. In the coldest weather, a tiny piece of breadflake, just covering a size 10 hook, takes some beating.

EXCAVATED DURING THE SECOND WORLD WAR FOR sand and gravel to build roads and airstrips, most of the old workings found throughout Southern England beside major river systems, have matured over the years into extremely rich, beautiful tree-lined fisheries. Those with a prolific growth of soft weeds, massive concentrations of zooplanktons and clear water, represent to the specialist bream angler what Everest represents to the mountaineer: the ultimate challenge.

Clear water pits which contain low densities of bream and lack aggressive competition species such as carp, breed the largest bream of all: those bronze-backed monsters in excess of the magical 10 lbs barrier. Throughout the spring and summer months their distinctive, blackish forms may be seen cruising steadily through the crystal clear water, as they gorge themselves on zooplankton and bloodworms from the rich layer of organic silt which has accumulated over the years.

DUE TO THEIR ENORMOUS DEPTH AND THE FACT that bream like to 'layer', line bites are unfortunately par for the course when summer ledgering. In particular the males (easily identified by the white spawning tubicles covering their noses), seem totally oblivious to the diameter of even a 6 lbs line. The answer of course, on those rare occasions when the bed is clean and without weed from the bank to the feeding shoal, is to sink the line along the bottom contours and actually fish with the rod tip sunk two feet beneath the surface. Alternatively, placing the bait on the very outer perimeter of the shoal's feeding area or patrol route, helps to minimise 'liners' whenever weed beds drape the line between bait and rod tip. Because the 'hot spot' is forever changing as the shoal browses from one area to another, the only solution is continual casting and retrieving.

Paradoxically, when fishing in rough conditions, when the bream cannot be visually located and when they do not characteristically 'porpoise' in the surface film enabling the angler to pinpoint their position, line bites are indeed a comforting occurrence, a sign that contact has been made. It is then a simple case of reducing range by a few yards each cast, until liners are eradicated. With luck only positive bites should follow. Strangely, the choice of bait is one of the least considerations. These bream usually respond to simple offerings like breadflake, worms, corn and cocktails.

So, is it all worth it? Of course it is. Enigmatic and beautifully coloured, the big bream is probably the most desirable of all trophies to the freshwater fisherman. So treat it carefully.

CLEAR WATER PITS OR LAKES RENOWNED FOR producing exceptionally large bream, invariably have the capacity to throw up equally large tench. The golden rule for this is: 'less competition, bigger specimen'. But still waters do not have it all their own way; clean rivers in which competition for food is minimal, can also breed some fine bream, the prerequisites being the same: a rich food source and a lush habitat in the form of extensive soft weedbeds and marginal rushes or sedges.

However, river bream are not so easy to catch. They are more astute, probably because they group in much smaller shoals, and strangely, their preference is for well-oxygenated, fast water. Weir pools in particular are well-known big bream hot spots, and quiver tipping a static bait on the bottom in a deep run is the technique for such locations. A big lob worm on the hook, in conjunction with loose fed casters packed into a block end feeder, is a magical combination, with bread-flake running a close second. During winter floodtime the shoal may roam into shallow, slow areas such as backwaters, or into the mouth of a side-stream where they can be caught on the waggler and a bait slowly dragging the bottom.

River bream produce noticeably less slime than still water fish. Perhaps because they are continually on the move, parasitic infestation is minimal and they therefore require less protection. Only the argulus (freshwater fish louse) is a regular passenger, but then if the angler looks really carefully, he will notice that every mint-condition river fish plays host to at least a few of these flat, transparent parasites.

INDIAN ADVENTURE

BETWEEN TALL MOUNTAINS PARCHED BROWN BY the sun, an Indian river cuts and cascades through black bed-rock. It runs into deep, turbulent pools where kingfishers sip the mineral richness; through deep gorges and over breathtakingly beautiful natural weirs, where the rock has been carved by the force of the river for millions of years; through wide, sandy flood plains where herdsmen water their goats, and through terrifying rapids. To contemplate the capture of huge fish from such an environment is to face the angler's consummate freshwater challenge.

The green habitat beside the river of prickly bushes, tall grasses, tamarind and mutti trees in which eagles and vultures perch, is lush only because once a year the entire lower valley is swallowed by the water of the monsoon rains which increase the river's depth by 30 feet or more. Inhabitants of the river include crocodiles, snapping turtles and exotic warm-water fish of every shape, colour and size imaginable. It is also the home of the legendary mahseer, a fish so large and powerful that its fight can only be described as awesome.

INDIAN ADVENTURE

A SEASONED MAHSEER FISHERMAN WITH NUMEROUS SPECIMENS ALREADY under his belt, Andy Davison scrambles quickly across the treacherous, jagged black rocks in pursuit of an unseen monster. In true mahseer form, it sucked up the small barbel like deadbait from the smooth glide immediately above the rapids, instantly dropping downstream into the maelstrom of foam and white water below. In one incredible run, 150 yards of 40 lbs test is ripped from the multiplier before the beast stops, to sulk down on the bottom behind a huge rock. Accompanying Andy, trusted guides Bola and Suban do the impossible. They courageously wade across 10 knots of white water, untangling the badly shredded line, as they follow the mahseer's route downstream through the hidden rocks.

WILSON'S ANGLE

NEARLY ONE HOUR LATER THE 6/0 HOOK STILL HOLDS. A FURTHER THREE blistering, careering runs take the intrepid trio still further down the rapids to where the river runs deep and narrow. At last the great fish tires, only minutes before Andy's back breaks. The guides leap into the flow as the mahseer's immense girth, unseen throughout the fight, suddenly appears on the surface, its mouth wide open, a totally spent force. Quickly, a soft nylon rope is made into a retaining stringer and threaded gently through the gills so that the monster's head can be held beneath the fast water where dissolved oxygen is greatest. Only when the catch is fully recovered is it taken to a suitable spot for weighing.

INDIAN ADVENTURE

CLOSE INSPECTION OF THE MAHSEER'S ENORMOUS mouth, with its thick-rimmed lips and long barbels for locating crabs and fishes, indicates that it is a massive breed of barbel, despite its carp-like, fully scaled body. Having beaten a giant mahseer, extra strength must be summoned to hoist it carefully onto the scales, wrapped in a big sling.

INDIAN ADVENTURE

IT IS DIFFICULT TO TELL WHO IS THE MORE exhausted after a long and memorable mahseer battle, the conqueror or the vanquished. But cradling 80 lbs of enamelled muscle, over five feet long and with the girth of a pig, for the camera does take some doing. Harsh shadows created by the Indian sun must be taken into account and the trophy turned first this way then that, before the photographer is completely satisfied. This is what takes a man half-way across the world to a strange land, to sweat for 24 hours a day, to live on a spartan diet of rice and peas, and to risk life and limb.

Battles have been known to continue for several hours and for as many miles down river, and after all that, the conclusion is not always successful. But epic scraps will be told time and time again around the fire, long into the night, by the few fortunate and strong enough to encounter mahseer. These are stories about fish which show no mercy, which strip the reel bare instead of sulking behind a rock while the angler regains line, or fish which crash over steep rapids flowing away from the opposite bank, necessitating a dangerous swim across swirling currents whilst clutching the rod. Tales are told of coracle rides through boulder-strewn white water where only the short paddle of your guide and his gritty experience lie between the possibility of landing an unseen monster, or being very seriously hurt. By comparison, the world of big game fishing in the world's oceans, from the safety of the fighting chair, seems a tame one indeed.

INDIAN ADVENTURE

WHERE ELSE BUT IN INDIA COULD THE FISHERMAN stand, legs submerged in warm water with tiny tropical fish nibbling at his toes, and glory in magnificent sunsets whilst patiently waiting, not for salmon, but for the real king of freshwater.

No doubt salmon stalwarts everywhere would testify in court that nothing could ever hold a candle to their fish. Yet, pound for pound, there is not an angler alive who, having caught both species from similar environments, would not rate the mighty mahseer crown king of them all. The beauty of the mahseer is breathtaking and the sheer physical power, durability and stamina of this creature is quite staggering. Even on substantial tackle, twice that of the salmon fisherman's, fights lasting over half an hour to subdue mere 20 pounders are commonplace.

The mahseer shares with the salmon the urge to migrate up river to spawn, usually during the monsoon rains, but unlike the salmon it never enters salt water.

WILSON'S ANGLE

ALTHOUGH MAHSEER LACK THE VISIBLE TEETH OF MOST PREDATORS, HIDDEN in their throat tissue are powerful pharyngeals the size of a child's hand, used to crush the large crabs and fishes upon which they feed.

A popular local bait for mahseer is called *ragi*, a paste made from millet flour which is first kneaded into balls with water, and then boiled for 30 minutes. This process brings out the natural gluten in the flour, making the bait rubbery so it stays on the hook in the strong currents. Whereas even a pound weight would bounce along the bottom, just an ounce of lead wire wrapped around the line, 12 inches above the bait, will hold when deliberately snagged among the rocks, until a mahseer wrenches it off.

INDIAN ADVENTURE

AS THE MAHSEER FISHERMAN COMES QUICKLY TO appreciate, India is a land of intense experience and stark contradictions; full of colourful creatures, strange perfumes and tastes and diverse exotic cultures. Death is never very far away – 10,000 people a year die in India from snake bites alone – and the cruelty of life is often shocking to western eyes. But it is these contradictions which draw the visitor back. Nowhere else has such a magnetic pull. The wildlife of India in particular is the stuff of rich memories for the fisherman, because he sees so much: wild monkeys taking food from the hand, elephant herds roaming the river valley, vultures waiting patiently for an ailing creature to draw its last breath. Brahminy and pariah kites cruise the thermals high above as you cast, and when darkness looms the cowardly jackals and hyenas sidle up to the camp for leftovers. The bold, dusky river tern is a frequent sight as it dive-bombs fish eagles who dare to invade its territory, as are otters who play close by. At daybreak there are a thousand prints in the sand, reminding you that there are still more river users – wild-boar, buffalo and leopards that come silently to drink and then disappear unseen into forest.

FLY RODDING

NON-ANGLERS THINK THAT FLY FISHING IS ONLY for trout and salmon. But anglers who relish the pleasure of using a fly rod, are not limited to flies alone, nor simply to the freshwater game fishes. Even small inshore species such as mullet and mackerel, when caught on a fly outfit, knock the spots off any trout of the same size. In reality, some of the world's most spectacular salt water fishes, bone fish, sharks, tarpon even sailfish, are regularly caught by fly rodding in the tropics, using some interesting techniques pioneered by American sports fishermen.

Most of the creations tied to catch these monsters bear little resemblance to standard wet and dry flies, but this is unimportant. The principal aim in fishing and consequently in fly rodding, is to have fun. So, provided it can be thrown with a fly rod, any type of plug, spoon, spinner, jig, fly, even a small dead fish, becomes the attractor.

Presenting a small, hackled dry fly in a chalk stream to a wary brown trout requires watercraft and skill, but no more than using the fly rod to propel a small spinner 20 yards across swirling rapids in search of arctic grayling. The concept is the same, so why not enjoy both challenges?

FLY RODDERS MIGHT ARGUE OVER WHICH IS THE most beautiful sight: the indescribable colours of an arctic grayling, or the majesty of a tarpon tailwalking away from the boat? Colours may be caught by the camera, but rarely is the sense of excitement. Think therefore, of a tropical swamp miles inland from the influences of salt water, almost a freshwater environment, where great sedges and reeds contour the marshy shoreline. There the fly rodder's punt is silently and skilfully steered by a guide to within casting distance of dark shapes which are slowly bow waving beneath the mangrove branches. With an alerting 'plink' the bucktail streamer touches down five feet to the side of the lead fish. Before the angler has stripped the lure more than a couple of yards, the tarpon is upon it, and in a lather of spray and flared gills the calmness of the silent swamp erupts into a spectacular floor show.

WHILE DACE AND GRAYLING PROBABLY CONSUME more shrimps than aquatic flies, the trout's favourite is the sedge. As the sun at the end of a summer's day sinks below the western sky, the sedge flitters and furrows the surface. Even during a chilly breeze such a hatch can prove exciting. But when they dance during a perfect sunset attracting trout to the surface which have been hidden up all day, the humble sedge, or caddis as it is better known to non-anglers, brings sheer delight to every fly rodder.

At a certain light-level, great gaping mouths appear from nowhere in oily swirls and the moth-like sedges disappear one by one. An accurate cast to a fish sucking in all within its path, brings immediate response. A lift of the rod, not too hard, as the line tightens across the calm surface is met with solid resistance. Coils of line on the ground amongst moist grass are ripped through the rings followed by the reel, screaming like a stuck pig, as the trout dives. The backing knot clangs through the tip ring along with 10 yards of braided nylon. Suddenly the line slackens and up, high out of the water, leaps a big rainbow, arching its body in acrobatic defiance of the hook wedged firmly into its jaw hinge.

ALL THE WORLD'S WATER IS OPEN TO THE TRAVELLING FLY RODDER — BE IT A mountain stream, a put and take fishery, or the Canadian outback approachable only by float plane. Here, huge-headed lake trout put a memorable bend in the stoutest fly rod, whether casting big streamers from the shore or twitching a leaded jig behind a boat drifting with the wind.

Incredibly, just a few ounces of carbon laminate can subdue the largest of fishes. The secret is in the fly rod's full curve. A never-ending elastic band to which even the strongest tail must eventually yield. Patience and confidence in a sound, well-balanced outfit, are the prerequisites for a happy ending to those long, exciting fights.

WILSON'S ANGLE

IT IS A SAD REALITY THAT IN PARTS OF BRITAIN, PARTICULARLY IN SCOTLAND and in the chalk streams of Southern England where the brown trout reigns supreme, her ladyship the grayling is considered a second class fish. On the other hand, in the unbelievably blue, clear alpine rivers of Austria, they are rated way above the trout.

Within the arctic circle the grayling is one of several sports fish; so the fisherman makes up his own mind. Strangely in these cold, turbulent waters the arctic grayling (identical to those in Europe, except that it grows to over 2½ lbs, with 5 pounders being quite common), repeatedly jump, putting up a better acrobatic show than most trout. In these wild waters their predatory instincts are fully developed, so tiny spinners, miniature sinking plugs fished fast across the current, will sort out the larger specimens.

FLY RODDING

USING THE SPRING OF A FLY ROD TO PROPEL SMALL spinners or lead-headed jigs demands rather specialised, well-matched tackle, especially if you wish to enjoy consistently long, easy casting without danger to flora, fauna or yourself. Soft-actioned rods and double taper lines for instance, are no use whatsoever. A fast tip carbon rod possessing some bulk in the lower half is essential, matched with a bass bug or salt water taper line, where all the weight is right up front close to the lure. This permits both line and lure to shoot through the air accurately and together, instead of fighting each other 15 yards apart, as would be the case with a double taper line. At a pinch, any weight forward line can be doctored to perform almost the same function by cutting four to six feet off the front end prior to adding the cast. This brings the thicker, heavier part of the line into play much earlier. To further reduce the distance between the forward taper and lure, use a much shorter cast than you would for general fishing. Opting for a larger diameter reel than is actually necessary, packed well out with braided backing, increases casting performance because as the line comes off in larger coils, it has less 'memory'. Whenever pike are expected, use a 6″ trace made from braided alasticum or 30 lbs mono with a size 12 swivel at the cast end and an American snap at the other. This allows both side to side movement and rapid changing of the lure. Though there are times when because of restricted casting distance fly rodding seems rather lacking, for the sheer fun of hooking and playing most species of freshwater and estuary fish, there is no finer outfit.

CONSIDER THE PROBLEMS OF HIGH SUMMER CHUB fishing: overgrown streams and rivers where only inches of clear water exist between weed and the surface. Save for floating crust or wasp cake on freelined tackle, such difficulties just happen to be tailor-made for the fly rodder. Bushy patterns of dry flies, palmers, mayflies, slow sinking nymphs, big buzzers, even miniature floating plugs – fly rodders can experiment with them all. There is also a static way of enjoying the sport. Add 10 feet of 10 lbs line to a regular fly outfit with sinking line and tie on a snap tackle. Mount either a small deadbait or half bait, and flip out a few yards from the boat or shore. When the bait touches the bottom, tighten up leaving a slight bow in the line, and when a pike finds the deadbait, the reel will suddenly screech into life, and you are playing a lively winter pike on two ounces of carbon. Unorthodox it may be, but you can't beat it.

FLY RODDING

THE TROUT IS EVERYMAN'S FISH. IT GIVES YOUNG worm danglers the thrill of the wrenching bite of a shark, and provides pensioners with a meal for the table. In chalk stream beats it offers sport affordable only by the privileged few. It brightens up the match fisherman's day when nothing else is biting. But catching trout one after another on trotting tackle quickly becomes a non-event.

The natural beauty of a wild fish straight from a fast, cold river, is caught here by the camera, and by comparison, a stew-fed stockie minus tail and pectorals, is a pitiful creature to behold. The trout is both stunning and sad. It is bright, but never seems to learn; strong, but after the fight pitifully weak; it is costly to catch, but its life is cheap.

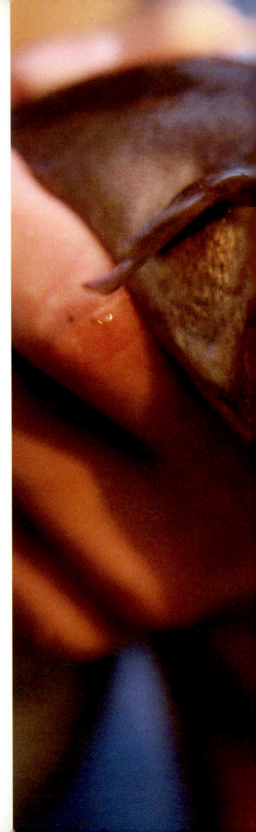

BOTTOM DWELLERS

'WHAT MONSTROUS EYES YOU HAVE' SAID THE fingerling roach. 'All the better to see you on the darkest night' replied the eel. 'You see, we bottom dwellers spend most of our lives in the dimmest light, down here amongst the mud, leaves, lily roots and all. We need sharp senses and instant reflexes, otherwise we'd soon go hungry' he continued. 'And what's more, we eels aren't as daft as most fishermen take us for, why do you think so few of us are caught by pike fishermen? We can easily distinguish a wire trace from monofilament, and as for those ghastly treble hooks – all we do is nibble away at their deadbaits – only the fresh ones mind – and leave them the skeleton. Sometimes I can hear their cursing from all the way down here. . . . That's my home under there' the eel added, nodding in the direction of an old galvanised dustbin lid while nonchalantly sucking in a juicy titbit.

The Londoner struck automatically as the waggler slowly disappeared. 'Think I'll have this one tonight, boiled in milk' he said to himself, slowly lowering the fat eel into an old sack and cutting the line. Not bothering to remove the single maggot and size 20 hook from its throat.

BOTTOM DWELLERS

THE CHANNEL CATFISH IS ONE OF THE MOST INTERESTING OF NORTH American freshwater species, and highly prized as a fighter. This is why each spring and autumn, catfish enthusiasts from far and wide flock to Lockport Bridge Dam on the Red River just outside Winnipeg.

Twice a year, thousands of big trophy channels in the 20–30 lbs range migrate up to Lockport, where simple ledger methods take them using fresh fish steaks cut from a shiner, a small white bass or a gold eye. Hooks are size 2/0′ barbless, gently nicked into the steak leaving the point well clear.

These cats are quite likely to pull an unattended rod right out of the boat, but equally they can be cagey. The most effective technique is to give only a little slack line while they mouth the bait and bore off, just in case they drop it, before striking hard and far back to set the hook. Then all hell breaks loose.

DOWN ON THE BOTTOM, IN THE THICKEST OF coloured water, the channel catfish will never have trouble finding its way about. Big, bad, and decidedly ugly, this beast is fitted with a formidable array of eight whiskers, or feelers, sprouting from its head. These highly sophisticated navigational aids also afford a horrifying last vision for its unlucky prey. Its rear-end, with deeply forked tail and adipose fin, is reminiscent of several game fishes. The cavernous mouth lacks pointed teeth but there are bristly holding pads — not unlike pot scourers — in the roof of the mouth and just inside the lower jaw.

Whilst channel cats are reared commercially in the U.S.A. for their delicious flesh, fishermen who respect their fighting qualities and willingness to feed even during the heat of a bright summer's day, are most conservation-minded, particularly where trophy-sized specimens are concerned. Strangely, young channel cats are almost silver grey and very much lighter in colour. They are also quite slender, hardly portraying the eventual deep, thickset form of the adult, which when provided with an abundance of food, can top 50 lbs.

WHEN BIG CATS AVERAGING 25 LBS APIECE SUDDENLY COME ON AND HIT, THEY arrive two or even three at a time. After an hour of nothing, save for the occasional dropped run or unwanted species mouthing the bait, suddenly and dramatically rods start bending. It is as though a signal has been given, summoning all cats back to work. Sudden changes in light values, the weather, air pressure or temperature might explain this, but it can happen bang in the middle of a calm, sunny day as if at the flick of a switch. Naturally, catfish anglers never complain, but it would be nice to ascertain exactly why they start feeding in earnest all at once.

It is a strange fact that in the U.S.A. and Canada, wherever the fisherman has a vast choice of species, the largest is not always the most popular, as it would be in the U.K., with pike and carp. For instance in Manitoba's Red River, along with the prolific head of channel cats and several lesser bullhead cats, there are walleye and white bass, plus an enormous and growing stock of common carp to over 40 lbs. The same river system in the South of England would instantly establish itself as the premier fishery in the country, yet at Lockport Dam the most popular species remains the walleye which average well below 10 lbs. This may be because of its eating quality and the fact that it responds to everything from artificial lures to cut bait. Channel cats, even the largest, come second, with the carp third or fourth down the line. A few nutters make sport of the carp by shooting them with bow and arrow, but nobody bothers specifically to catch them on rod and line. What a strange waste of an entire population of hard fighting fish which are numerous even in the 10 to 25 lbs range.

SPECIES LIKE THE BARBEL WHICH INHABIT FAST RIVERS, USE THEIR FEELERS OR whiskers, which have tiny paste pads at the very tips, to sneak down through sand and gravel in search of selected food items such as shrimps and crayfish. However, the danubian wels European catfish, now deliberately being stocked into selected land-locked British waters, not only has four sensory feelers beneath its chin, but a pair on top. In addition, from each corner of the enormous ear to ear mouth, is hinged a long, probing feeler, with 360° degree manoeuvrability.

OF THE SEVERAL TYPES OF BARBEL FOUND IN European waters, one particularly hard battler inhabits the deep, powerful waters of the River Ebro, which cuts through the Pyrenees before emptying into the Mediterranean on Spain's eastern coast. These Spanish whiskers shoal in vast numbers and weigh between 3 and 5 lbs, despite sharing the warm water of the Ebro system with giant catfish, American black bass, mullet, pike and incredible numbers of common carp.

It would seem to contradict the barbel's physical make-up to intercept suspended or trotted baits within four feet of the surface where depths can vary between 10 and over 30 feet, and the water is heavily coloured and running fast. Yet they are as aggressive off-bottom as they are down amongst the jagged rocks which cover the bed of the Ebro. Spanish barbel provide savage, unmissable bites to ledgered meat, corn or pastes, and if they turn downstream and the rod is not held fast, it will be dragged in.

Far more exciting, though much less accessible than barbel because it requires the solitude and perseverance of night fishing, is the spread of the danubian wels catfish along the River Ebro. Specimens in the 50 to 80 lbs bracket are now being caught with such regularity throughout the middle reaches where they were first introduced, that unparalleled sport seems assured for the future.

WILSON'S ANGLE

ON A WORLDWIDE SCALE, FRESHWATER BOTTOM dwellers come in an unbelievable variety of exotic forms. Flat headed, shark-like catfish, bulbous headed cats, armour plated cats, eels of every colour, diameter and length, and in South America even freshwater stingrays exist. Most are predatory customers, but a proportion feed on nothing but the nutritious green algae, spending their lives moving from one rock to another holding on by their unusual fully protrusible sucking mouths in the most turbu-lent of currents where the richest algae growth exists.

Such oddities as the Asian red carp, would provide wonderful sport if only it grabbed the angler's bait, because it is equipped with large powerful fins. But it is only when one is accidentally foul hooked on the trebles of a lure intended for predatory species, or becomes trapped in the mesh of a cast net used for gathering small fish as bait, that the fisherman gets to marvel at its beautiful coloration and strange pre-historic mouth.

THE AMERICAN INFLUENCE

UNFORTUNATELY, TO MANY FISHERMEN, CATCHING PIKE OR ANY PREDATOR simply means either live or deadbaiting. This is a great pity. Don't they realise that out there is a whole, new exciting world of artificial lures? Predators will snap at anything which happens to take their fancy. Whether they do this out of frustration, territorial aggression, genuine hunger or just cussedness no one knows. What's important is the fisherman wielding the rod and the pleasure he gets from his sport, his excitement, and his thoughts about the fish's underwater world.

Tempting predators with artificials is without question more difficult. It requires a much higher level of casting skill and general watercraft than tossing out a fish bait which, whether live or dead, does the work for you. Knowing the difference between the variations of each artificial is critical, so that the right pattern is chosen for the right purpose. Be it spoon, spinner, diving floater, diving sinker, spinning jig, buzz bait, surface popper, plastic worm or whatever, there is so much variety, so much to learn. Experimenting is fun, and British fishermen really do have the American influence, now growing yearly in stature, to thank for the advancement of the artificial lure.

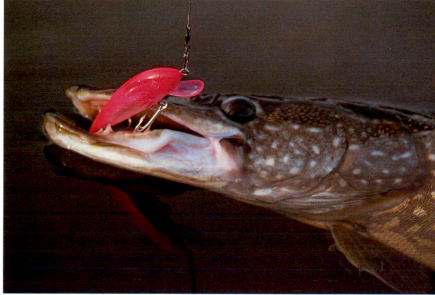

FOR THE TIME OF YEAR THE SHALLOW WATER IS unusually clear. Conditions are calm. Around and alongside the shorelines steeped in aldercarr, birch and goat willow, an assortment of floating and diving plugs are tried, but to no avail. Big fluttering spoons, spinner baits and diving wobblers are, one by one, systematically worked to aggravate the pike into action. It is as if there is not a single pike on the Broad. But the fisherman knows different. Eventu-

ally, a particular pattern, perhaps of a certain colour will bring a response.

And so it happened on this particular afternoon on this particular water. Suddenly on its very first cast a gaudy, fluorescent pink, shallow diver, just happens to have that indefinable combination for the conditions of the day. The surface is thrashed into a turmoil of spray and distorted colours as a pike bites into the plastic body and feels cold steel.

CAREFULLY RETURNING A FINE PREDATOR, CAUGHT using an artificial, is not only the final satisfaction, but an assurance of good sport in the future. Pike may have an armory of teeth, but they can suffer badly from inexperienced handling.

First there are those whose reel line is too light for the continual casting and retrieving demanded by lure fishing, who indiscriminately leave their costly artificials in a predator's jaw. Then there are those who, without thinking, insist on gaffing pike and puncturing their chin membrane unnecessarily. It is so much easier to lift even a large fish out with a gloved hand once it has been played to a standstill. A scared, inexperienced fisherman who by fluke manages to boat a monster and hasn't the slightest clue how to remove the trebles, both sets of which are caught in the fine mesh of the landing net, is an equal nuisance. Moreover, leaving it to flap about on the bare boards in the bottom of the boat removes the pike's body mucus which is a protection against parasites. Finally, there are those who fail to appreciate that leaving lures stuck on sub-surface snags without making any effort to retrieve them, constitutes a serious hazard to wildlife, particularly swans.

So the lure fisherman must at all times be responsible. For lures and lines dangling from trees or rushes; for rusty hooks discarded and not taken home to destroy; for the effect his presence has on fellow water users who do not take kindly to the summer plug fisher searching the lily pads, when they are trying to tempt carp on floaters, or crunching along the bank because he just happens to be enjoying a mobile method, without consideration for those sitting silently whilst static fishing.

This code of conduct may be unwritten, but it should be followed by all.

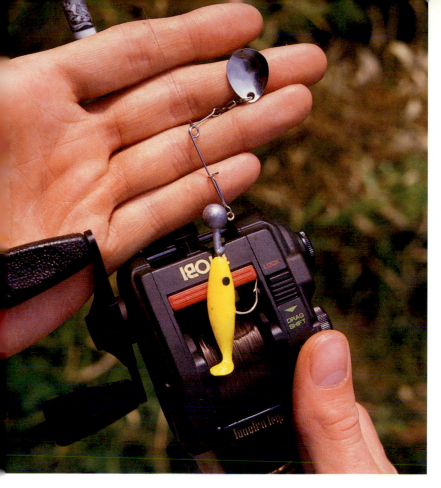

LUBRICATED PLASTIC WORMS, SALAMANDERS AND newts of every conceivable colour which feel to the human touch more life-like than the real things, have largely been created for the American freshwater bass fishing industry. They are intended for big mouths, small mouths and a whole family of sunfishes which, given the right enticement, will grab hold.

Whether mounted on a single hook and worked through thick weeds, twitched erratically through and over lily pads as the tail of a surface popper, or added to a spinning jig to provide that soft, natural feel to fool a cagey predator, plastic artificials really work. Not only pike, but also perch, zander, trout, salmon, grayling and chub all go for them. Enormous fun can be had by working these imitations on a single-handed little casting rod and baby multiplier combo. Compared to long spinning rods, which absorb much of the action created at the arm end, these stiff sticks really do give life-like movement to all artificials.

THE AMERICAN INFLUENCE

HUGE BROWN TROUT KNOWN AFFECTIONATELY TO SOME AS 'FEROX' AND 'mammoth', and unseen pike who enjoy a carefree existence in deep lakes, reservoirs, Irish or Scottish Lochs, have had it all their own way for too long. Gone are the methods of yesteryear, of heavily leaded trolling lines and of waiting till the beasts come up to the shallows for spawning. Modern downrigger trolling techniques, perfected in North America on the Great Lakes, coupled with the very latest in sonar equipment, provide the lure enthusiast with an effective armoury. What is even more important is that immediately the line leaves the down-rigger clip, the fight of that monster can be enjoyed on tackle as light or as heavy as the fisherman chooses.

WILSON'S ANGLE

IN A DESOLATE CANADIAN LANDSCAPE CLOSE TO THE 60th parallel, between a thousand islands spiked with black spruce, birch, red willow and jack pine, down in the cold clear depths reaching to 100 feet and more, lives a massive breed of lake trout. Their usual daily diet is a rich variety of white fish, lake herring, burbot and their own smaller brethren; but they also hit big vibratory spoons and and plugs trolled 30 feet behind the boat on the downrigger.

Heaving into a 20 pounder, hooked over 90 feet below, even taking into account the stretch in 15 lbs test, provides one memorable battle. Repeatedly the great fish dives, ripping 20 to 30 feet each time against a tight clutch. As it nears the surface its arching body and shaking head can be clearly seen through the pure water. Hopefully, the barbless hook on the heavy spoon will hold, though many monsters come adrift at the very moment when the trout finally breaks surface, leaving a frustrated fisherman and a disappointed guide.

THE AMERICAN INFLUENCE

BEFORE RETURNING IT TO THE COLD, CLEAR DEPTHS A FINAL MOMENT IS savoured to marvel at such a magnificent wild creature. Its long athletic frame is coated in a metallic varnish of miniature golden octagonals set in a rich background of pewter mosaic – a strange pattern of colour not dissimilar to that of the American brook trout. But there all similarity ends, because the tail of the 'laker' is truly enormous, easily twice that of commercially reared trout, and deeply forked with a distinct narrow wrist. There is a warm greyness about its secondary fins of which only the dorsal is not edged in white, though all are spotted and large. Char-like in its overall plumage, yet totally different in every other way, the 'laker' is a fish which tolerates only clear, cold unpolluted rivers and lakes such as are found in Canada's north-west territories. These actually contain more than nine per cent of the world's freshwater – in itself a staggering fact. In the province of Manitoba alone, for instance, there are over 100,000 lakes, deep and cold, most of them uncharted and unnamed, where caribou roam across the ice which covers the surface for over eight months of the year. This is the home of the giant lake trout, not simply a fighting machine, though in that category it has few equals, but a unique breed. Unique, because although 40 pounders are caught each summer once the ice melts, with the record standing at an incredible 65 lbs, these enigmatic fish are a relatively slow growing species.

It is small wonder that those who run even remote fishing lodges in Northern Canada, might appear a trifle over-protective in their desire to preserve the quality of their lake trout fishing. No longer are trophy sized 'lakers' taken back and hung up around the dock for all to see. A colour photograph provides the proof beyond all doubt, whilst the memory each fisherman takes back to civilization can never be erased.

WILSON'S ANGLE

LAKERS WILL HIT ANY KIND OF TROLLED SPOON OR PLUG WHICH HAPPENS TO give the illusion of a meal. They have even been known to grab in their huge jaws and then shake, the 10 lbs ball of lead to which the downrigger clip is fixed. On other occasions they can be frustratingly choosy, so the fisherman varies the size, colour and action until a successful combination is found. For conservation of these great fish, large single barbless hooks replace the standard trebles with which most large artificial lures come fitted.

THE AMERICAN INFLUENCE

ONE OF THE MOST EXCITING BENEFITS OF THE American influence, is the sheer diversity of artificial lures now finding their way across the Atlantic into British tackle shops. Yet ironically they do not necessarily attract the species they were originally intended to deceive. Take for instance those odd looking spinner baits comprising a vibrating blade and a skirted, leaded, single hook, mounted at each end of a V-shaped frame. Designed purely for the big and small mouth basses, spinner baits can, in the right circumstances, prove lethal for both pike and perch in British waters. In heavily coloured lakes especially, where artificials must be worked slowly with maximum vibration, there is nothing to match a large spinner bait. It is one of the few lures that can be retrieved slowly without loss of action, but is not the best of hookers when it comes to the hard bony surface of a pike's jaws. One remedy is to wire on a small treble behind the single, which has the added benefit of taking pike which hit short.

THE WORST . . . AND THE BEST

A HUNDRED YEARS FROM NOW OUR DESCENDANTS will say 'how could they have let this scourge of pollution ruin our planet?' World-wide the environment is being destroyed at a terrifying rate, seemingly with no thought for those to follow.

We anglers understandably have a deep personal interest in environmental issues because they directly affect our sport. The bloated bodies of dead fish littering the banks are fit only for rat food. Whether their death was a result of pig slurry, or industrial filth pouring from a waste pipe, it represents a disregard for the living world which will eventually affect everyone.

The world needs strong criminal legislation against polluters, now. Every country should instigate a national plan for arresting further damage, and as a watch-dog there is no one better placed than the humble fisherman. He is a constant monitor of the self-destructive society in which a succession of governments have, by not concerning themselves with long-term policies, sanctioned polluting practices. It is easy to blame governments, but it is public pressure and the watchfulness of the individual that will help to turn the tide.

WILSON'S ANGLE

IT IS A SAD REFLECTION ON THIS WONDERFUL SPORT, that anglers who are so often intolerant of other water users, can be their own worst enemies. There are those who show a callous disregard for the environment which has given them so much by leaving litter instead of taking it home. There are some who retain specimen carp and bream for too long, causing stress from which the fish may pre-maturely die. There is the limit bag trout angler who carelessly shakes off unwanted fish without ensuring that they have fully recovered and vacated the margins.

Of course such selfish sportsmen are a minority, but they should in common with all other water users, be encouraged to respect what is after all, the source of their enjoyment.

THE WORST . . .

BETWEEN THEM, THE HERON AND THE BARN OWL symbolise all the qualities that go to make a successful fisherman: stealth, silent movement, the ability to keep perfectly still, agility, sharp eyes, sensitive ears and a love of marshland. Simply to catch sight of a heron waiting in the early dawn offers a magic identical to fishing itself. The heron epitomises the essence of what drives every angler – the primeval hunting instinct. The only difference is that for the heron success is crucial, otherwise it will starve. The sports fisherman on the other hand, is simply playing the game.

In recent years as rivers have declined through water abstraction and farming practices, the heron's food supply of small shoal fish has been drastically reduced. Fewer fish for the heron also means fewer fish for the angler, but the heron is as adaptable as his human counterpart. There are rich pickings to be had from fast food joints such as garden ponds, trout hatcheries and well-stocked carp lakes. However, for all its apparent physical size, the heron normally weighs between 2½ and 3 pounds.

The barn owl is not as adaptable as the heron to a changing environment. Indeed, now that their traditional nesting sites such as old barns and hollow trees have become scarce, barn owls are an endangered species. Thankfully there are an increasing number of programmes for rearing young birds and introducing them into the wild, and people with suitable sites are encouraged to leave them untouched. However, it remains to be seen whether man's intervention can swing a balance which is at the moment tipped in the opposite direction.

WILSON'S ANGLE

RETURNING HOME IN THE STILLNESS OF A SETTING SUN AFTER A PERFECT DAY'S fishing will always have romantic quality. The soft but reflective colours, pink and beige, gold and orange, pewter and red, shift and change in form and density like a kaleidoscope till the coldness of night takes over, bringing down a cloak of mist. Fishermen learn to savour these moments with special silence, reaching for the hip flask to stoke the remains of their coffee while they stare in contemplation as the boat enters the wide estuary and heads up river on the making tide.

Later, when the tide ebbs, the wading birds start to appear, exploring long mud flats created by rich sediments washed down from river marshes and fields. Curlew, dunlins and oyster catchers peck, prance and squabble. On every square, oak marker post along the navigable channel sits either a gull or a cormorant. Theirs is a scavenging life, gleaning nutrition from the river's graveyard where only the like of eels, flounders and mullet exist in the muddy, brackish waters to interest the very occasional fisherman.

Bass might run a fair way upstream given the right tide and a following breeze off the sea, as will sea trout, in far larger numbers than most fishermen would credit. But who, save the local netsman who only ventures out under the cover of darkness, gets to taste their flesh? By nature such men are loners, short on words and patience with the questions of fools who they do not suffer gladly.

Only fisherfolk and the wildfowlers ever really get to know and love these estuarial marshes – men who live from the sand, not the land, whose knowledge of the tides, wind and currents is well beyond that which the average angler is willing to learn. This is not an occasional pursuit, but a way of life, which is why, save for fishing boats, the salt marshes remain lonely.

THE BEST . . .

SITTING ALONE IN A BOAT WITH A STORM WHIPPING UP, OR ENJOYING A SHORE lunch of fish caught, cooked and eaten within the hour, these are two experiences which provoke the same gut feeling in every fisherman. It is an ancient feeling of survival, of being at one with nature; knowing yourself, your limitations and what you really enjoy when alone with the world. The crackle of the fire and the smell of wood smoke awake long-subdued pioneering instincts and everything feels as though you were doing it for the first time. Equally potent is the sizzling of the fish as it cooks, and the aroma of coffee brewing. What meal indoors ever tasted so good?

THE BEST . . .

THERE ARE TIMES WHEN IN SPITE OF ALL THE ODDS BEING AGAINST CATCHING anything, you still venture out. There might be ice in the margins and the prospect of a bleak, barren valley, or heavy snowdrifts which merge the fields into a single landscape. There might be the comfort of a warm log fire, or a favourite old movie on the box tempting you to stay in. But despite all this you set off and, having arrived at your chosen spot, know it was worth the effort. The sense of expectancy, the eternal optimism of the fisherman, is what drives him out of the house and into the cold.

It may well be that a few casts will prove enough. You may settle for a lone bite, for one small fish, or for nothing other than to feel the cold in your body until your feet and cheeks can stand it no longer. However long or short your stay, the principal challenge has been satisfied.

The precise nature of the enjoyment that a fisherman derives from his sport is impossible to define. No doubt this is why non-anglers think us so strange. Some are never satisfied until a monster lies beaten at their feet; others become excited merely by a sucked maggot. Perhaps it is simply the challenge of the day that fixes the stakes, and since that challenge is always different, fishing represents an unending search.

Although fishing is largely dependent upon luck, no fisherman would ever admit to *feeling* unlucky. He might *say* that he is the unluckiest fisherman alive, but he can never afford to *feel* that way. The difference is slender, but sufficient to send the angler out when he doesn't really stand the remotest chance. Then, quite suddenly, when absolutely nothing is on the cards, the wobbled deadbait happens to clunk a stationary predator on the head: it is a jack pike lying close in to the bank, with not the slightest intention of feeding until the conditions change. Some meals are however, impossible to pass up. The rod tip knocks twice, and the angler, prepared to put caution to the wind, strikes instantly, lest the bait is dropped. Adrenalin courses through his veins and the bitter cold and lonely wait are instantly forgotten.

IN WINTER, FOR THE FISHERMAN WHO SEEKS HIS pleasure from flowing water, there will only ever be two fish. When it is freezing cold, and the river is completely out of sorts, and little else fancies feeding, the chub can always be relied upon. In snowstorms, in floodwaters, it remains the angler's true friend.

During the late afternoon, if the weather turns mild and the river is nicely coloured, there is no better time to hope for a grandad roach, one of those magical 2 lbs fish. As species go, this is a comparatively small fish, but it is the ultimate reward for a lifetime spent studying flow patterns and float control, and for being at the waterside when the mist rises at dawn to look for big roach as they characteristically porpoise on the surface (something they also repeat at dusk). For this is the open secret of the specialist roach angler: the crucial importance of pin-pointing the quarry.

Large concentrations of fish respond to trotting tactics using casters, maggots or bread crust, when conditions are right; whereas small groups of predominantly large fish are easily spooked by continual casting and retrieving. For them, a big lump of breadflake presented static on the bottom, following a little loose feed of mashed bread, is far more likely to succeed. Then patience plays its part.

THE BEST . . .

ONCE THE LEAVES HAVE FALLEN FROM THE BROADLAND SCENE OF ALDER, CARR and water-logged birch trees, can there really be anything more exciting as winter approaches, than experiencing the brute physical power of a big pike repeatedly crash-diving for freedom, sending up great sprays of water against the anchored boat? While the pike's metabolic rate is still racing, before low water temperatures halve its fighting qualities, such battles may continue for several minutes against sounds from the screaming clutch. Many a carp fanatic would indeed be surprised by the quality of such a contest, and by the fact that pike can pull so hard and move so fast.

You should concentrate your efforts before any prolonged bout of sub-zero weather sets in, because afterwards winter pike never really pull as hard again until around the end of March when the thermometer starts to climb. In conditions of extreme cold, pike invariably take a long time to turn and swallow, irrespective of the size of the bait and of whether it is live or dead. By complete contrast, during the prewinter period, even a big deadbait such as half a mackerel or a whole herring will be wolfed down instantly.

Seeing how the sliding float nonchalantly sneaks across the glassy surface before slipping under, or the way the line shoots in a blur through the rod rings, really gets the adrenalin pumping. Is it finally the big one, or a scrappy 5 lbs jack? Unfortunately you can never tell. Folklore has it that slow confident runs are to be had from the largest, pot-bellied females, and the racers are courtesy of immature fish. However, those with a string of big pike under their belts know that there are no hard and fast rules. One thing is absolutely certain, pike have the ability to bring out the hunter in each and every fisherman.

143